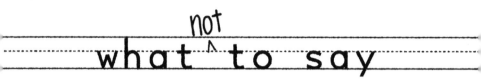

what ^{not} to say

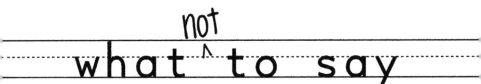

what ^not to say

Tools for Talking with Young Children

SARAH MACLAUGHLIN

Bay Island Books

Published in the United States by Bay Island Books
P. O. Box 485, Corte Madera, CA 94976

Text copyright © 2010 by Sarah MacLaughlin

Illustrations copyright © 2009 by Patricia Krause
To contact the illustrator online, go to www.trishkrause.com.

Printed in China on acid-free paper

PUBLISHER'S CATALOGING-IN-PUBLICATION DATA
MacLaughlin, Sarah.
        What not to say : tools for talking with young
    children / Sarah MacLaughlin.
        p. cm.
    Includes bibliographical references.
    LCCN 2009911720
    ISBN-13: 978-0-9654694-2-5
    ISBN-10: 0-9654694-2-5

        1. Child rearing.   2. Parent and child.   3. Child
psychology.   I. Title.

HQ769.M33 2010   649'.1
                                              QBI09-
600217

Contents

Let's raise children who don't have to recover from their childhoods.

— Pam Leo

Where to Begin

What NOT to say? Adults with responsibility for one- to six-year-olds have enough to do without worrying about the finer points of language! Why pay so much attention to what we say? Because ill-chosen words are at the heart of most negative interactions with kids. Being mindful of our words, and how they are said, is vital for a child's well-being. How adults talk to kids greatly influences who they turn out to be. It's as simple and as important as that.

The 66 expressions presented here are among the most common we use with children. Some of these may be in your repertoire—or Aunt Alice's—and some you wouldn't dream of saying. Of course this collection isn't exhaustive. We adults can always come up with more! After you've read the chapter introductions and discussions of the "don't say" sentences, you will have a framework for recognizing other detrimental things said by you and others in a child's world.

Some expressions that are counter-productive will resonate with you right away and it will be easy to drop them. Others may fall away more slowly. We all have those "uh-oh" moments. If you catch yourself saying something ineffective—or worse—don't be hard on yourself, and remember that awareness always precedes change. Rather than dwelling on occasional poor form, focus on your intention to improve.

Just as important as recognizing harmful language is knowing what words to use instead. Young children can be very challenging, so it's helpful to have clear ideas about what to say when they push our buttons or do something outlandish. I offer many specific suggestions for how to say it better. When one approach doesn't work, try a different one. The plan is to fill up your "bag of tricks" with verbal and behavioral responses that get results.

The first step in using clear and positive language with a young child is gaining awareness of what you are really communicating, through not only words but also body language, actions, and tone of voice. Send the right messages by modeling behavior you want and using words and a tone you'd like to hear back. Even the child who is too young to talk is paying close attention and storing information about what you say and the way you interact with him and others around you.

Likewise, children communicate to us through not only words but everything they do. Part of our job as grown-ups is to figure out the message when there are no words. Sometimes it's an expression of interest, for example, a toddler who may be thinking, *That lamp cord looks so appealing I want to grab it.* Other times it's a feeling, a need, or both: *I'm tired and need to take a nap* or *My brother is getting all the attention and I want some.* If you can decode what may be motivating a child, it will help you understand his actions. You can then respond in a more understanding and productive way.

Children often exhibit behavior that baffles us. Aggression and emotional outbursts are familiar territory for anyone interacting with young kids. The following chapter introductions and discussions offer new ways of looking at these issues and creative approaches to talking about them. If you're mired in power struggles, I'll lead you to more peaceful ground. Looking for new ways to guide a child toward healthy habits? I have advice. Take the suggestions one at a time, and don't be discouraged if you don't get instant positive results. Making these changes is a process, not a prescription. If you want to delve further into any area that is discussed, look through Resource Books for Grown-ups at the end of the book for some excellent reading choices.

As well as reading about children, reading *to* them is invaluable. Good children's books can have a positive effect on behavior and change a child's understanding of the world. For a young child, even a preverbal baby, regular reading aloud is a habit I encourage. Characters in a story provide a great way to explore important topics such as kindness, common fears, and even death. Books also enhance language skills and allow adults to offer little ones focused attention and a diversion that instantly calms and corrals them. A difficult situation can often be ended by simply saying, "Come over here. Let's read a book." Excellent children's books related to the chapter topics are suggested throughout.

Little kids are messy and silly, frustrating and wise. Raising a child, or just spending the day with one, can be a real adventure. Bring your flexibility and patience—and don't forget a sense of humor. These qualities, and using the right words along the way, will promote understanding and a peaceful atmosphere. And you will enjoy your time with children more.

1 Why Do I Say That?

Reasons we say the wrong things

We want to treat children well but often miss the mark by saying something that just doesn't work. Out comes an old stand-by or a critical blast of frustration. When we say ineffective or inconsiderate things to children, it doesn't mean we are bad people—there are reasons why.

How we were raised   Unthinkingly we parrot what our parents said because we heard it so often in childhood. Some classics like "Don't be so sensitive" are passed down from parent to child. With other sayings, each generation comes up with new ways of expressing the same ideas. Your grandmother might have said, "You'll be the death of me"; your dad put it, "You're giving me gray hair"; and now you say, "You're stressing me out!" Too often such automatic expressions are meaningless or even harmful to young children. Have you ever said, "You are such a pain"? If you then thought, *I can't believe I just said that,* you've already taken a big first step.

Fatigue and stress   At times what we say is a matter of the quickest, easiest way. Adults give knee-jerk responses because we are worn down—kids can sap so much of our energy. When they keep asking why they can't have something or do something, it's easy to defend your "No" with "Because I said so." A harried teacher or a mom who is on call day and night might dismiss a fussy child with, "Just cut it out!" If you hear yourself saying these things, it's a clue that your own needs for adult conversation or rest are not being met.

Current trends Ways of speaking to children that follow cultural patterns can wear thin. For example, "Good job!" is repeated so often nowadays that a child becomes deaf to the message. Or adults might try to emphasize current attitudes, such as children now being expected to be heard as well as seen, and repeatedly say, "I hear that you ..." An overly permissive parent can get into the habit of saying, "OK honey, if that's what you want." Mindlessly parroting these popular phrases is a path to nowhere.

Fear Many adults are afraid, afraid of harming children emotionally or provoking temper tantrums (no fun!). In general, parents, teachers, and caregivers are more worried than in the past about making mistakes, or causing children to get angry or unhappy or become alienated. When it happens, we may feel guilty or inadequate. But of course no child grows up perfectly happy. Applying the techniques in this book will help you say the right things and create harmony in children's lives.

Who hasn't said these?

Who is responsible for this mess?

Picture this: small children playing in a room strewn with objects of every size and description, and an angry adult looming in the doorway. Since the answer to this question is probably, "All of us," asking in this way is confusing. It also carries an implied threat that one child will be singled out and made responsible. Try to check your anger and address the disarray directly: "This is an awful mess! It is not okay to take out *all* the toys when you play. Put some away." Or maybe the situation is that childhood classic, crayon art decorating the walls. You can take the crayons away and ask the "artist" to assist with clean-up. As the grown-up, who presumably wants things kept reasonably clean and neat, it's your job to supervise messy activities.

READING TIP:

The Tale of Two Bad Mice by Beatrix Potter. Ages two and up. These two mischievous mice make a big mess, but for all the right reasons.

What on earth are you doing?

This common question really means, "You are doing something wrong." Young kids always keep us on our toes because, as fairly new human beings, they have quite a lot of learning to do. Toddlers will assault others, ruin property, abuse a pet, or put themselves in danger. Instead of asking a meaningless question, just describe what you see. If you come upon a child giving the dog a haircut, talk about it: "I see that you've cut some of Rosie's fur off. That's not okay, and she could have been hurt. Don't do that again." In a situation like this it's often hard to keep our cool. If that's you, just take the scissors and walk away to regain your composure. When a child is heading for danger, yell "Stop right there!" or "No!" Use a forceful, loud tone. Saving a shout for a situation that warrants it makes it all the more effective.

READING TIP:

Alexander and the Terrible, Horrible, No Good, Very Bad Day by Judith Viorst. Ages three and up. Trouble follows Alexander all day, but his mom understands that sometimes that happens.

Do as I say, not as I do.

This is a prickly situation to address. Remember that your actions speak louder than your words. Young children will mimic behavior they see regardless of what they are told. Instead of this overworked demand, give them an explanation that states the limit clearly: "I know you see *me* put on lipstick, but it's for grown-ups only. It is not for you to wear or play with." Take the time to childproof and keep forbidden things out of reach. If you as parent or caregiver are setting a poor example, it's best to acknowledge the disparity in rules: "You're right. I drink sodas sometimes and yet I don't allow you to—that must not seem fair. Soda isn't healthy for anyone, but it's especially bad for kids' growing bodies."

READING TIP:

When Mommy Was Mad by Lynne Jonell. Ages two and up. Little Robbie is a masterful mimic.

Because I said so.

We resort to this staple when a boy or girl won't stop making demands. While such a non-answer may not be damaging, it's curt and dismisses the child's feelings. It hinders a loving connection between adults and little ones. A similar and often used line is, "Because I'm the grown-up, that's why." This may work when a child is three but is hardly a permanent solution. It's more productive to keep open communication with children from an early age, even if this means extended conversations about family or classroom rules. When a difficult situation arises, explain your reason clearly: "We are not going to stop for ice cream because it's late and we're heading home for dinner." If a child persists you can say, "I'm not going to change my mind about it."

In lots of places children are starving, so you'd better eat your dinner.

What a child eats for dinner doesn't affect whether or not children elsewhere in the world have food. But this old saying evokes guilt, and eating out of guilt is hardly enjoyable. No one can *make* a child eat. It's perfectly normal for a growing boy or girl to skip a meal now and then, or to prefer sweet potatoes over liver. Allowing children to serve themselves at meals can help—the child gets a say about what he puts on his plate *and* it's less wasteful. You can still encourage healthy eating by asking, "Do you want another bite of peas? They are so tasty." If he refuses, don't push to the point of a power struggle. Mealtimes can be pleasant, but not when there are battles over food.

READING TIPS:

I Will Never, Not Ever, Eat a Tomato by Lauren Child. Ages one and up. An older sibling uses creative words to encourage his little sister to try something new.

The Seven Silly Eaters by Mary Ann Hoberman. Ages two and up. A family full of picky eaters finds a way to satisfy everyone.

Green Eggs and Ham by Dr. Seuss. Ages one and up. Sometimes you think you don't like it, but try it and you just might.

Be nice.

"Be nice" is something everyone has heard and repeated to children, but a child doesn't know what to do with it. Instead of asking for *nice*, describe the desired behavior and use more understandable words like *kind* and *friendly*. For example, say, "Use a different, gentle voice to talk to me." You can send a clear, nonjudgmental message this way: "You are hitting me and it hurts. Stop that." This reflects your feelings and gives an instruction. Set a boundary where it's appropriate: "You took Jane's book from her and now she's crying. If you don't give it back, we will leave." Follow up with reinforcement: "You are not treating Jane with respect. This tells me it's time to go."

Reading Tip:

> *Bootsie Barker Bites* by Barbara Bottner. Ages two and up. Bootsie and her playmate just can't get along.

Don't even think about it.

This popular warning is a real head-scratcher for the younger set. When it does work and stops a child in her tracks, she is probably responding more to your tone than your words. If a child is approaching kindergarten age and worth her salt at arguing, you could hear, "I wasn't thinking about anything" or, "I don't know what you're talking about." This might start a quarrel that could easily be avoided. Simplify your message to a straightforward request: "Please do not touch that wet paint." In this case your tone of voice is useful—low and authoritative can work wonders.

2 Change Your Words, Change a Child
Making it work

A typical scene: It's time to leave the house and my toddler starts kicking when I try to put on his shoes. "Liam, please stop that," I say. Liam continues to kick. I answer his defiance with "Liam, please stop it. We need to put your shoes on NOW!" He keeps struggling. I repeat myself but don't notice that a pleading, demanding tone *(pleeeeze, just do it)* has slipped into my voice. That tone can be taken as a challenge, and a child's resistance will likely continue. Now I'm really irritated and raise my voice. Flash forward to a crying child and me coming unglued—shoes, of course, still not on. Sound familiar?

This frustrating scene may seem like a typical, even normal, interaction. Yet if adults can change their perfectly natural reactions, it can change a child's actions. When dealing with unwanted behavior, what often comes to mind is something negative like scolding, threatening, or spanking—time-honored approaches based in fear. There are other, far more effective ways to give guidance and structure that also allow children to feel safe.

Simple as One, Two, Three

The most important strategy for influencing behavior change is talking to these small human beings respectfully. You'll always win with this trifecta: firm, kind, and consistent. Even when you need to say "no," acknowledge the child: "That pill bottle you found makes a cool noise when you shake it. But it's not a safe toy, so I'm putting it away. Let's find something else you can play with."

One of the best ways to guide children's actions is an old stand-by: request, remind, reinforce. Start by making a request, and include the reason for it: "Please play gently with your trains. I don't want them to break and the noise is hurting my ears." If this request is ignored, ask again and include the consequence for not complying. "If you continue to bang and crash the trains, I will put them away. This is the last reminder." Remind only once before taking action. When kids test adults over and over, repeated reinforcement can be exhausting. However, the reward of consistent follow-through is eventually doing less reminding (or nagging) about the desired behavior.

Changing the Way We See

Sometimes not talking to children about their behavior, but simply adopting a different perspective, is the most effective approach. The technique of reframing can magically shift you and a child out of a negative situation. There are four "frames" to use for seeing children in alternate ways.

1) Instead of reacting as usual, try reframing the child developmentally. This means being aware of a child's stage of development. How should a two-year-old, as opposed to a three-year-old, react to bathing, or being carried, or any other common activity? Knowing a child's developmental milestones can take the edge off adult frustration about certain behavior in little ones. The norms for a child or student group should be reviewed every six months or so. A good resource is the perennial classic *Ages and Stages* by Karen Miller. Recently I reframed the persistent testing of a three-year-old in my care, who constantly yelled "Go away!" Remembering the nearly universal and *unrelenting* negativism in children of his age allowed his parents and me to better tolerate this, and to set limits in a firm yet loving way.

2) Reframe the rules—both the number of rules and their requirements. Boundaries for kids should be based primarily on safety and respect. If there are too many, you can be sure that most rules will be tested and plenty of them broken. With only a few firm rules, kids have less to remember. Standards should also be appropriate for an age group. To expect toddlers to pick up after themselves, sit quietly through a long meal, or obey complicated instructions is not realistic.

3) Reframe a child's environment. Teachers often do this when there is trouble in a classroom. If kids go helter-skelter to the playground, structure can be added by using squares of carpet for lining up, and a routine that includes stopping at certain places. At home, baby-proofing rooms and reorganizing them in a kid-friendly way will reduce time spent managing problems. If a child is running up and down a hall or through the house, try rearranging furniture to eliminate the racetrack.

4) Reframe a child's temperament. Doing this can help adults refine their guidance for boys and girls, and better support particular needs. Children differ considerably in how active, distractible, social, and sensitive they are—there is no "right" way to be. A highly active child thrives on more physical stimulation than one who is naturally calm. A child who "switches gears" slowly will benefit from extra time for transitions. Children whose temperaments are recognized by adults have an easier time accepting themselves. These girls and boys will have more enjoyment in their education and upbringing.

Changing a Child's Attention

Another useful technique is redirecting. This simply involves guiding a child's attention away from testing, demands, or other tiresome behavior. Redirecting works particularly well during the preschool years, when adults can creatively engage a child's imagination and avoid hassles or a hard-line approach. For that three-year-old who wouldn't stop yelling "Go away!" I sidestepped my annoyance and calmly asked, with a conspiratorial twinkle in my eye, "Where would I go?" Together we imagined various places until I was outside in the snow. I looked at him wide-eyed and announced, "I would be sooo cold!" He found this imagined power of his a delightful possibility, and dropped the demand to "Go away!" Other types of redirecting are to tell a story, offer a book, or suggest a different activity—water play is always appealing—or a new setting: "Let's go outside!" Acting goofy and using ridiculous voices, exaggerated drama, or role reversal are other approaches that children usually respond to enthusiastically.

With a scenario like Liam and his shoes the strategies of reframing and redirecting would have helped me be more patient. I could have reframed developmentally, remembering that Liam's timetable for moving from one activity to another is typical for a two-and-a-half-year-old, and allowed him an extra ten minutes or offered a brief period to squirm or dance. Or I could have redirected his attention by telling a story about The Little Boy Whose Shoes Never Fit Right, and later slipped them on easily as part of the plot.

The Benefits of Narration

Describing what I see or hear, narration, is my favorite way of talking with children about their behavior, work, and ideas. With this approach there's no need to berate kids or send them to the naughty chair. Without using language that judges or shames, narration sends a clear message and social information that a child needs. Consider these two statements:

"You are hitting your sister."

"You cleaned your room all by yourself."

It's easy to imagine how your tone of voice and facial expression would convey whether or not you want either thing to happen again. When a child's action is undesirable, add a limit-setting directive. "You are hitting your sister—stop that," is clear and concise. When an action is desirable, no additional feedback is needed.

Speaking in a matter-of-fact tone defuses a situation when emotions are running high: "You're throwing food. Stop that or get down." "You got mad about the doll house and pushed Vivian over. She fell and now she's crying." The key is to say enough so a child understands what is socially unacceptable without feeling ashamed for behaving inappropriately to begin with. Narration also gives a child the opportunity to reflect on an incident and to come to some conclusions about right and wrong.

Another narration technique is to relate what you are doing. This gives kids information that allows them to correct a problem on their own, though it does require a lot of patience. For example, standing by the car while a toddler squirmed boisterously in his car seat, I have said in a neutral tone, "You are wiggling and I can't buckle up your seat. I'll wait for you to stop." Or you can just engage with the child, perhaps saying, "Oooh, you've got the wiggles! Me too! Let's wiggle our arms and wiggle our legs. It's wiggle time!" A minute later "wiggle time" will have lost its appeal and he will likely be ready to move on. Then you can fasten that car seat and go.

Redirecting Our Focus

The electronic age may have increased our productivity, but it has put a damper on communicating with young children. Now it's possible to catch up on e-mail at the playground, chat on the cell phone while pushing a stroller, or listen to tunes on the iPod during playtime. Not to mention the distraction of television and computers at home. All of these things decrease our interactions with kids, who need to be really listened to and responded to.

Talking with children, and singing, asking questions, and reading to them using eye contact and facial expressions, are an essential part of their intricate process of learning to talk. Even a preverbal child benefits from Dad's conversation about what he sees while walking down the street. Baby might hear, "Look at those squirrels scurrying around" . . . if Dad isn't on the phone. Since communication begins as soon as a child is born, talk to your baby whenever you can. When we turn off the electronic devices and focus on children, we give them the invaluable gift of our full attention, which will undoubtedly have a positive impact on their behavior.

All of these approaches do work. They are simple but require patience. You may have to change ingrained habits, and that isn't easy. Yet once you start making small changes, your relationship with kids will improve and—another big payoff—their behavior will too.

Some words really sting

What's the matter with you?

Because a small child's view of the world is so self-centered, this reaction to misbehavior only intensifies that. She may think, *I don't know, maybe everything!* A critical question is likely to leave children feeling defective, unfixable. It's better to respond to each situation specifically without questioning a child's character. If you found your three-year-old cutting up her new pants with wild abandon, you might assume that something had indeed gone wrong. Take the scissors away, but then back up for a moment before accusing her. Recently she was playing in the sewing room while you used *your* scissors to cut fabric for a pair of pants. The reason for her actions is now a bit clearer. Remain calm and restate the boundaries: "Your scissors are for cutting paper, and only when a grown-up is there."

Sometimes there's no reassuring explanation for children's behavior—they just like to experiment. That's small consolation when a budding scientist drips glue onto the cat's fur! Talk about why this was not a good idea and clean up the kitty together.

I hate you, too!

If a young child says, "I hate you," this unexpected retaliation is hurtful, and worse, the child just might believe you. At an early age children learn that *hate* is a strong word, and using it gives them a sense of power. Kids will say shockingly negative things as a test rather than a true reflection of what they believe. Try not to discount or manipulate a child's feelings by responding with, "You don't mean that" or, "I'm going to cry now." A sensible reply to "I hate you" might be to consider the motive: "You said you hate me because you really wanted that toy, and now you're angry and sad because I said no."

READING TIP:

Mean Soup by Betsy Everitt. Ages two and up. Horace has a bad day but his mom offers a good solution.

Good job!

It seems like this statement would be nice for a child to hear. But research shows that in the long run praise, which is actually a form of judgment, can be ineffective and sometimes damaging to children. The child may believe he only does well at certain things and therefore is no good at others. It also sets the stage for him to always try to please others, to become dependent on feedback from adults. This robs him of the opportunity to truly please *himself,* which is the foundation for gaining self-esteem and self-motivation.

Many parents today are enthusiastic cheerleaders for their children. Mom or Dad claps like a seal and gushes over the child who has just stacked four blocks or gotten his pants buttoned up. A big or contrived reaction can give kids the message that certain behavior is excessively important. If you do give praise or encouragement, be sure it's genuine and specific, not general. Really pay attention to a child's activities; look when he yells "Look at me!" Instead of mindless praise, use narration and a positive tone: "I see you, Jonah. You climbed to the top of the tower!" Instead of your evaluation, comment on how the child might be feeling: "You did it yourself—you must feel very proud."

I told you so.

An adult who says this sounds more like a sibling mid-squabble than an understanding parent or caregiver. As with "I just knew this would happen," it condemns a child for not having foresight. When there's a mishap, grown-ups should be aware of a child's intention—perhaps he was trying to help—and try to see the humor, if any. If food has spilled, take a deep breath and state the obvious: "Oh no, there's food everywhere!" Instead of pointing out how he messed up, talk about what happened: "Jordan, it looks like you couldn't keep your plate steady, so I'll take it the rest of the way to the table. Some of your food spilled—let's clean it up." For growing children, mistakes are valuable teaching tools. Allowing kids to learn from their experiences is a great philosophy, but it can be challenging to practice—especially if there's a messy accident!

This is all your fault.

It's normal for young children to be self-centered, and they may readily believe that things are their fault—news coverage of Hurricane Katrina reported some children blaming themselves for this natural disaster. When things don't go right, give kids clear feedback about their behavior and share your feelings with them: "I am frustrated that we are late to our appointment. Next time, we will go the first time I tell you we need to leave." If you allow a child to distract you from leaving on time with his activities or preoccupations, it is actually your fault.

"Now I get a clean room star!"

Show Grandpa how you can count to ten.

Asking a child to exhibit his latest skill is something many of us do without thinking. When my nephew was about nine months old, he learned to shake his head on command. It's a wonder the baby didn't develop whiplash from the number of times various adults prompted him, "Shake your head!" We were thrilled that he could understand our words and make the necessary connections in his little mind. No one considered whether this would inhibit a desire to learn new things for himself. But over time, if a child is repeatedly asked to perform his "tricks," he may lose his natural motivation to master new things on his own and only perform for the sake of pleasing an audience.

Requesting a show from a child and then showering her with praise does her no favors. If you acknowledge new learning with narration, it keeps a child grounded in her own capabilities as opposed to being dependent on your approval. "You just counted to ten!" along with a smile, sends a clear enough message. Grandma, siblings, and caregivers will be in the loop about new abilities in due time. No special emphasis needed.

3 | What Do Children Hear?
Our confusing language

There are many ways we confuse children when talking to them. English is loaded with potentially bewildering words, idioms, and expressions that carry meanings quite different from their strict definitions. Adding to the confusion, young children are so literal. When a child is asked to "lend a hand," does it mean he's supposed to take that hand off? A little boy in my care once crouched down and slapped the ground after I suggested, "Let's hit the road." It's easy to forget that these familiar turns of phrase sound strange to children who are only just learning to speak the language.

Sometimes misunderstanding occurs when a child doesn't hear slight differences in word pronunciation. One source describes a little girl's fear of the "mean ducks" in her ceiling. Trying to figure out where she got this idea, the family finally traced it to a contractor who had pointed to the ceiling in the toddler's bedroom and said, "You've got bad ducts."

Slang, sayings, and exaggeration can puzzle the younger set. Until they absorb language irregularities, common slang like "Cool" or "Give me a break" will likely be misunderstood. If you tell a toddler, "Don't spill the beans," he probably won't understand that it's about not sharing information. Around age three, children begin to grasp the "sayings" concept and often love the silliness of them. You can help young children by explaining perplexing language, for example, "'It's raining cats and dogs' is a saying that means it's raining really hard." Exaggerations can be silly, too ... or simply make no sense. What do toddlers think when you say, "I've told you a thousand times"?

Kids may be surprised to learn that many words which sound alike have different meanings—pairs like "pea" and "pee," or "aunt" and "ant." For years I thought my grandmother Ceil was named after a marine mammal. The popular Amelia Bedelia book series helps kids with words and expressions that have double meanings. The spirited housekeeper Amelia misunderstands directions like "Draw the curtains"—and pulls out a sketch pad. Added to these language challenges are sarcasm, euphemisms, and rhetorical questions—they usually go right over young kids' heads. Explaining them can keep you on your toes: "You're right, I didn't sound grateful when I told that man, 'Thanks a lot.' He wasn't helpful and I was being sarcastic, saying the opposite of what I meant. I didn't really mean 'Thank you.'" The amazing thing is that kids eventually do absorb many of the hidden meanings in our confusing language.

It's our natural tendency to talk to young children in language that mirrors their own. The occasional "I'll kiss your ouchie" or, "It's time for night-night," is fine, but in general try to use proper words and a normal tone. "Does my wittle baby need a baba?" doesn't help a toddler learn the English language. Referring to yourself in the third person instead of using pronouns isn't beneficial either. Saying *Mommy* instead of *I* or *me* is an odd habit we easily fall into, one that can be confusing for a child. Remember how literal young minds are, and pay attention to your words and their meanings.

Truth or Consequences

Although most miscommunication with young children is unintentional, some is not. In many situations our inclination is to lie or sugar-coat the truth. We do this to protect children, mostly from information we think they shouldn't know or can't handle, such as death and divorce. When important facts are hidden, children sense it and tend to imagine terrible things—usually worse than the actual situation. Adding to the harm, a child might worry that the reason for not telling her is that *she* is the cause of the trouble—young children are naturally self-centered.

If, for example, a couple going through problems in their marriage does not address this in some way with their child, she will recognize the difference between the telltale signs of stress and her parents' efforts to "put on a happy face." Instead, the situation should be discussed in language a child can understand: "Daddy and I have been fussing at each other lately, the way sometimes you and your brother fight. But we're talking to work it out, just like you're learning to do." Sometimes in an effort to protect kids from the truth, we hurt them even more.

What exactly do we mean?

How many times have I told you not to do that?

This rhetorical question makes no sense and is an unproductive way of speaking to a child. If you use the R's—Request, Remind, and follow through with Reinforcement—you won't need to ask this. Address annoying repetitive behavior with something like, "I have asked you twice to stop banging that toy around, so now I'm taking it away for the day. Next time please listen the first time. I know you can do it." This clearly restates the requested behavior and offers encouragement too. Kids will learn to listen the first time if you consistently follow through and don't give so many "chances" to listen.

You're driving me crazy.

For young kids, this may bring to mind scary ideas of someone wild and out of control. It also implies a warning: *You are pushing me to my limit and I'm about to lose it.* Instead, make a direct statement about behavior and expectation: "Running in the house and throwing pillows must stop right now. Find something calmer to do." Offer an alternative activity, such as sitting at the table with crayons and paper for a while. Track the times of day a child "acts up." If there is a pattern of disruptive behavior, try to head it off by presenting a fresh activity. Building in periods of focused attention may curb a child's troublesome behavior.

READING TIP:
Olivia by Ian Falconer. Ages one and up. This lively character is loved by all, even if she sometimes wears her mom out.

It's time for your bath, okay?

Adults are talking out of both sides of their mouths with this common expression. The "okay" part is not meant, no matter what comes before it. If the child were to answer "No," would you say, "All right, Aisha, we'll skip the bath tonight."? Be clear about your expectations and don't confuse the issue by tacking on this question meant to persuade. First, be respectful of the child's wants and needs. Give her a heads-up about what is about to happen: "Aisha, in five minutes it will be time for your bath." Engage her in the activity by asking for her help: "Please get your pajamas out so they are ready once you are all clean."

READING TIP:

No More Baths by Brock Cole. Ages one and up. Any child will want a bath when she gets this dirty!

I'll be back before you know it.

Not only is this promise unclear, it's unlikely to be true. I have consoled many preschoolers as they've waited for a parent to pick them up. Instead of saying "before you know it" or "in a little while," tell him how long you will be gone or when you will return, and encourage him to enjoy himself: "José, I am going to leave you for the morning and I'll be back to pick you up at 12:30 after lunch. Have fun with your friends."

Separation can be hard for young children—trying to gloss over this fact just makes it harder. Many parents don't realize how much their little ones look to them for guidance when separation happens. If you trust the caregivers your boy is being left with and behave accordingly, he will pick up on that. Don't hesitate near the door, look back longingly, or gush about how much you will miss him while you are gone. Actions like these are a sure sign of your own discomfort. And if *you* aren't comfortable about leaving, why should he be?

READING TIP:

Carl Goes to Daycare by Alexandra Day. Ages one and up. Madeleine goes to daycare with her helpful dog Carl.

You scared me to death!

This melodramatic statement invokes a scary scenario that is disrespectful to a small child. The word *death* is also confusing when you are obviously still alive. Be honest and clear about your feelings if a child has done something that frightens you, and say what is expected in the future: "Running into the street is very dangerous—a car could have been coming and hit you. I felt very scared and that's why I yelled and grabbed you. We have to hold hands every time to cross the street."

Fluffy was sick, so we had her put to sleep.

Using "sleep" to mean death can only be frightening for a small, literal-minded child. Be straightforward and say instead, "Fluffy died last night. She was very ill and suffering and the animal doctor could not make her get well. He gave her a shot to help her die so she would not suffer any more." Then answer any questions and listen carefully to the child's reaction, perhaps sharing your own thoughts about what you will miss about Fluffy.

Adults often project onto young ones their own anxieties about death, or steer clear of the topic altogether. Try using experiences with death as teachable moments. If you encounter a dead animal on a walk, use this to spark a conversation, likewise for attending a funeral or making a trip to the cemetery. Speaking openly with children about death is a great gift to them. Discuss the fact that bodies can give out when they are sick, injured, or old, and also that some aspects of death are unknown. Children usually embrace the notion that certain things are a mystery.

READING TIPS:

The Fall of Freddie the Leaf by Leo Buscaglia. Ages one and up. This wise book illustrates how death is a normal part of life's cycle.

The Tenth Good Thing About Barney by Judith Viorst. Ages three and up. A family works through their grief about their pet by remembering his wonderful attributes.

Be a big boy.

This is very confusing for a little boy! *How am I supposed to get bigger?* he might well ask himself. Even if he understands that the request is about more mature behavior, not physical size, it's still unclear. Instead, ask for what you want: "Please keep your food on the plate during dinner."

The plea to act like a "big" boy or girl is often used during toilet learning. If you want a child to go, make a direct request: "Will you climb up and sit on the potty for a minute?" A teaching concept called "scaffolding" comes in handy here. Like the steel structures at building sites, this means guiding progress while allowing a child to do things on his own. Scaffolds for toilet learning might be making sure the child has easily removable clothing, and asking him to teach a doll or stuffed animal to use the potty. (There are specialty dolls for this purpose.)

READING TIPS:

Toilet Tales by Andrea Wayne Von Konigslow. Ages six months and up. Which animals know how to use the toilet?

Bigger by Daniel Kirk. Ages three and up. A young boy assesses how much he's grown over the past years.

4 | A Child by Any Other Name ...
Labels and nicknames

A child by any other name is not the same. When a child hears a word or phrase applied to him often enough, it "sticks" just like a name tag. This can change his self-image. Children tend to accept without question the labels adults use to describe their physical characteristics, personality, abilities, and limitations. No single word can define a child, but young children cannot grasp this sophisticated concept. As they grow, their beliefs about themselves are influenced by the adults around them. Diane, often called Angel, tries to live up to her nickname and that might seem like a good thing. However, nicknames and labels pressure children to act a certain way instead of being themselves—sometimes well-behaved and kind and other times unruly and vindictive.

It is easy to be unaware of the impact of our descriptive words. "Be good" you might say to your little one as you drop him off at kindergarten. *Aren't I good? What does that mean?* he might wonder. *How will I know when I'm good enough?* If such clear-cut thoughts don't occur to a child, he could still be building a case against himself, or trying to figure out whether he is "good" or "bad."

Adults tend to use positive labels to encourage children in a variety of activities. This is an ideal opportunity to try narrating instead. Words that help without limiting are best. Consider each parent's language in the following scenarios.

James at twenty months is fearless on the toddler-oriented playground. His father barely takes his hands off him and James struggles for independence to scoot quickly around the nearest structure. As James climbs, Dad says, "Be careful son, this pirate ship is very high. You are such a wild boy. Watch your head! Good boy. Hold Daddy's hand, please. Good boy. What a bold boy you are!"

Sophie is the same age. Her mother watches closely as the little girl negotiates the playground. Mom is careful to stay nearby, but doesn't hover unnecessarily. She moves in if she sees Sophie traversing a drop-off point, or signaling for help. She also talks to her daughter: "Sophie, you are doing it all by yourself! Last week you asked for help in that spot. Reach ... you did it. Your muscles are getting strong."

The father's verbal cues are warnings, labels, and praise. Sophie's mother gives a different sort of feedback by narrating her daughter's movements and comparing them to a previous playground trip. Both parents want to keep their children safe, but their words send different messages about each child's capabilities. In turn, these words influence the child's behavior. James picks up on Dad's nervous hovering and may defy him in an unsafe way, or act more fearful. Sophie will probably increase her skill and self-confidence, in part because of Mom's descriptions.

If a child is told he acts a certain way, he will tend to continue, even if the description is negative. Is it helpful to you, or a child, to joke about him being a slowpoke? We often use unflattering labels to differentiate children, saying things like, "He's our little show-off," or "She's the troublemaker in this classroom." Obviously adults don't want to reinforce these behaviors, but what about the more subtle labels? For example, consider "tomboy," an outdated stereotype for a girl who is athletic, or doesn't fit old ideas about girlish behavior and clothes. When a word like this pigeonholes a young child, she may feel there is something wrong with her. You can comment in a nonjudgmental way on a girl's or boy's preferences: "Jenny loves to climb trees and play soccer. She's very active." Or, "Eddie likes quiet activities—playing with dolls and trucks and looking at picture books."

The labeling phenomenon is much like downloaded information. When we are young, we hear certain things being said to and about us, and they are stored on our hard drives. As we get older, those old files may continue to show up on our screen—and they are terribly hard to delete. Remember that the descriptive labels we apply to children can affect them for a long time, maybe even a lifetime.

Labels that limit a child

You are such a little liar.

Raising an honest child or upholding the truth in your classroom is a worthy goal. Since honesty is the childhood character trait that's most important to many parents, we tend to get very upset when children are dishonest. But don't assume a child has the moral compass of a scorpion if you catch him in a lie. Lying is a normal childhood milestone as children learn to avoid the truth for fear of getting into trouble. If a child has an accident or breaks a rule, encourage him to own up to it: "I can see why you wouldn't want to admit that you got paint on the couch, but I'd like for you to tell me when something like this happens. Let's clean this up—and remember that paint must always stay in the kitchen." Give him reason to trust you by keeping your cool and not focusing on the lie—a big negative reaction will only lead to more lying in the future. When children are punished for lying, they don't become honest, they just become sneaky.

Sometimes children's untruths are just a testing of their story telling abilities. Here are a couple of good responses to tall tales: "Sounds like you have a good imagination" or, "I think you made that one up."

In their groundbreaking book *NurtureShock,* Po Bronson and Ashley Merryman note that children have great difficulty distinguishing between a "white lie" and one that is more serious. Once children understand that white lies are told to spare someone's feelings, which they are encouraged to do, they interpret this to mean always saying what they think others want to hear. When this happens, respond to the situation and not the fib: "You said you hung your jacket in the closet, but I see it here on the floor. You must have wanted to hang it up, so go ahead and do that now."

READING TIPS:

Ruthie and the (Not So) Teeny Tiny Lie by Laura Rankin. Ages three to six. Ruthie lies, but eventually does the right thing and tells the truth.

Cloudy With a Chance of Meatballs by Judi Barrett. Ages two and up. Grandpa tells a bedtime story that's a very tall tale—or is it?

What a good girl!

When I hear, "Good girl," or "Good boy," I half expect to also hear "Sit! Nice dog." Aside from the fact that these phrases sound like obedience training, they are vague and overused. No child is entirely "good" or "bad" and either label puts limits on children. Some parents use praise to encourage desired behavior. Narration is also very effective. For example, "You remembered to stop and hold hands before crossing the street." Perhaps include a simple statement of gratitude such as "Thank you, I appreciate that."

READING TIPS:

Good Boy, Fergus! by David Shannon. Ages one and up. The family dog has a wild day.

Dear Mrs. La Rue: Letters From Obedience School by Mark Teague. Ages three and up. Mrs. La Rue's dog tries to get her to see things from his perspective, then saves the day.

That was a stupid thing to do.

Telling a child that she did something stupid is equivalent to saying she is stupid—hardly what a parent or caregiver wants to convey. Instead, narrate the problem and direct the child toward a solution. For example, "You stuck a bean in your nose. Try blowing into this tissue and maybe it will come out." Further questions allow a child to think about the problem herself: "We might need to go to the doctor for some help. What do you think?"

Even if you don't say the word "stupid" first, your three- or four-year-old will likely come home from preschool with some charming new vocabulary that includes this gem. When it happens, don't stoop to her level or make a big deal out of it. (That's true for a lot of unwanted childhood behavior.) Using a matter-of-fact tone will defuse a child's powerful excitement at "getting your goat." Have a chat about what "stupid" means—addressing a word directly can take the charge out of it.

READING TIP:
   Pigs by Robert Munch. Ages two and up. The pigs seem dumb, but are they?

You're being a crybaby.

Linking "cry" and "baby" implies that only infants should give way to tears. This is both unreasonable and unkind. The crybaby label stems from outdated rules in our culture about even small children controlling tears, especially boys. Just as with laughing, crying is good for either gender. Gradually this is becoming more socially acceptable. Recent research has shown chemical differences between tears brought on by peeling an onion and tears caused by feelings. Emotional tears are found to be naturally cleansing, the body's way of releasing toxins and stress.

When crying fits are used to manipulate, giving a child clear limits may reduce such outbreaks. "You can cry until you are ready to stop, but we will be leaving the park in five minutes. So if you want to play, now is the time." It is also possible to comfort a child without giving in. For example, "I see you are frustrated and crying because you didn't get to pick out a toy today. Would a hug help you feel better?"

READING TIP:
   Baby Brains: The Smartest Baby in The Whole World by Simon James. Ages one and up. This baby knows a lot, but when he's far from home he misses his family.

You're so bossy.

Some kids are naturally more outgoing or assertive than others. Watching a child dominate another child, or a group, can be hard—adults want to encourage fair behavior. But unless a child is hurting another, it could be best to not intervene. Allowing children to work out their own power differences and minor squabbles is good practice for them. There are ways to help children "balance the scales" without using any labels. Redirecting them toward cooperative play is one option: "Jamie, try stacking the blocks with Susie and see what the two of you can build." Or attempt to draw out a child who seems passive: "Ellen, do you want a turn being the teacher too?"

READING TIP:
   Let's Be Enemies by Janice May Udry. Ages two and up. One child is bossy but these two friends work out their differences after all.

You are a little terror!

Or "tornado," or "wild child." We may use these as terms of endearment for young ones who blast through the living room like whirling dervishes. There is something fun and entertaining about the unbridled frenzy some kids can sustain for unbelievably long periods. That's the problem. This behavior can be cute . . . for about five minutes. Unfortunately, a two-year-old is just getting started at five minutes, and kids are much better at winding themselves up than winding down. Also, this label can become a self-fulfilling prophesy. To a child, what sounds like positive feedback encourages behavior that to an adult becomes quickly annoying.

Make sure that a child with a high need for physical activity is given lots of opportunities to expend energy. If you want to curb wild behavior, use clear requests such as, "Stop running in the house," and "No yelling indoors." Involve young children in setting up house or classroom rules (refined by you) based on what kind of environment they want.

READING TIP:
   Where the Wild Things Are by Maurice Sendak. Ages two and up. There is a time and a place for being wild. Max ends the day safe and warm in his own room.

You're acting like a sissy.

This criticism, usually directed at boys, is as outmoded as the term "tomboy." It implies predefined gender roles and encourages a child to suppress natural feelings and reactions in an effort to appear "strong." Acknowledging a child's true feelings fosters self-acceptance and self-confidence, which supports him on a path towards true strength. When a child is fearful, narrating is helpful: "Aaron, I see you closing your eyes and turning away when the ball comes to you. Do you want to practice with a softer ball?" Be supportive about aversions and let children proceed at their own pace: "It's okay if you don't want to pick up that bug. I'll hold it for you if you want to just look at it."

READING TIPS:

Jack Quack by Lucy A. Nolan. Ages two and up. This duck is nervous, but he gets what he wants in the end.

Anna Banana And Me by Lenore Blegvad. Ages three and up. Anna Banana's bravery inspires this little boy.

Don't be a smart aleck.

A young child probably does not know what this means. The dictionary says it is "an obnoxiously conceited and self-assertive person with pretensions to smartness or cleverness." Without understanding the put-down, a child will still hear the tone of disapproval. The label might give him more mileage than you'd like if he accepts it as a symbol of power. He may think, proudly, *Daddy is annoyed because I'm a smart aleck!* Instead of name calling, be a good model for the children in your care and ask directly for what you want: "Please talk to me in a different tone," or "Rewind and try that again. I don't respond well to that voice." Both of these requests are also useful when children are whining.

READING TIP:

The Grouchy Ladybug by Eric Carle. Ages one and up. A smart-mouthed ladybug has an exhausting day being grouchy.

5 | Do What I Say, or Else
Threats and bribes

It's a common belief that threats and bribes are must-have tools for adults—the staples of child rearing! These methods are popular because they do work. Threats manipulate a child through fear—of a certain punishment or withdrawal of something cherished. Bribes are typically snacks, treats, and toys, and they send the message that you don't have faith that a child can succeed without extra incentive. Threats cause him or her to fear you. Influencing behavior in these ways is not only unnecessary, it is ultimately harmful.

Threats intentionally make a child feel that he or his belongings are in danger. Often this is conveyed by both tone and words, as in the familiar expression "You'll be sorry." Instead of scaring a child, caution him about the natural consequences of his behavior: "If you dump the paint out, you won't have any left." When the consequence involves action from you, it needs more explanation: "If you keep throwing sand, it could hurt the other children. So if you do, we will leave the park to keep everyone safe."

Always follow up with the consequence, but make sure your expectation is age-appropriate. Consider changing a child's surroundings to eliminate the need for input from you. If you insist that a child stay within eyesight, physical barriers like gates might be necessary to help keep him corralled. Toddlers will feel the pull to explore regardless of verbal directives, so create an environment where they can succeed without constant adult feedback.

If kids are offered bribes to elicit good behavior or a new achievement, this establishes an unwise precedent. Bribes detract from the natural satisfaction that children gain from their accomplishments. A child's ultimate payoff should be mastery of something, whether it's a behavior like sharing toys, or a new skill such as learning to swim. When you want a child to do (or not do) a certain thing, it's more productive in the long run to simply say what you want, then give positive recognition (or not) when the result occurs.

How do rewards, both material and symbolic, fit into the picture? Rewards, like bribes, are pervasive in our culture and very sought after. Think of the elementary school talent show where the adults in charge devise special categories so every child can take home a ribbon. Many people use prizes and achievement charts to instill good habits in children. While these can sometimes have a positive effect, using such methods regularly is counterproductive. Rewards given too often tend to create the same problems as bribes. Occasional and temporary rewards work best, and only until the new skill or behavior is learned. Sometimes a spontaneous and unexpected reward can help create the atmosphere of cooperation you want: "Everyone did their work without complaint on chore day. Let's go play mini-golf tomorrow to celebrate!"

In her handbook *Connection Parenting,* Pam Leo suggests that children continue to be uncooperative and resistant only if they have unmet needs or unexpressed hurts. She believes that children will behave well when they feel connected to and understood by the adult taking care of them, eliminating the need to use special influences. Narrating and questioning can help. Both you and the child can benefit if you address a child's behavior directly, talking calmly at eye level and offering compassion. You might learn about a rough day at preschool if you say something like, "You keep hitting your sister when you know it's hurting her—that's not like you. Are you unhappy about something?" After his feelings have been expressed and acknowledged, he will likely stop hitting because he no longer has the urge to vent. Keep in mind what the child might be trying to tell you with his behavior. Remembering this can guide adults to respond with thoughtful words rather than threats or bribes.

Words meant to manipulate

You'd better stop that by the time I count to three.

This old stand-by can be effective because it evokes fearful or anxious feelings. It also sets up the potential for testing and defiance. Instead of using the deadline routine, stop what you are doing, get down on the child's level, and just say what you would like to happen. Asking for help instead of being coercive can bring out accommodating behavior: "Will you help me put these books away? There are so many! Let's count them as we do it." Or try a creative approach tailored to the situation, for example, "Drum on this pillow instead of on the cat."

To practice listening skills, try occasionally playing the "freeze" game, where you put on music and kids freeze when the music is turned off. "Red light, Green light" is another entertaining exercise that makes stopping actually fun for a child. These kinds of listening-stopping games can help children learn to moderate their body movements and follow directions better.

I'll give you something to really cry about.

This mean-spirited statement, with its threat of physical punishment, undermines the safe environment that you aim to create. It carries a double whammy because it's usually said to a child who is already distraught. If you have lost patience with a child's crying and carrying on, simply say so: "Joan, I can tell you are still very upset because you broke your favorite doll, but I am tired of listening to such loud cries. I am here to listen, comfort, or talk when you have calmed down." If this situation occurs in a public place, you may need to leave because you cannot force a child to stop wailing. In fact, I have found that efforts to do so may escalate a child's distress. Sometimes kids who are stuck in a groove of wallowing in emotion can be redirected by a song or other attention-getting approach.

If you say that again, I'll wash your mouth out with soap.

The latest twist on this old-school approach is putting hot sauce on a child's tongue as punishment for offensive words and back talk. I find the idea of putting unpleasant things in kids' mouths, well, distasteful, and downright abusive. Physical punishment of *any* sort sends the wrong message.

First, adults need to provide a good example. Don't use language or a tone that you find unacceptable with children. Granted, that's easier said than done! A friend recently confessed to me that because of her own carelessness, her two-year-old's favorite new expression was "f*#!ing dog." Second, try the low profile approach. Ignore the first offense—kids often try out expletives for their shock value. Or ask inquisitively, "What does that mean?" This may stump kids because they often don't even know. Be clear about the rules you want them to follow: "Your mother and I believe that 'damn' is a bad word, so say 'darn' instead."

A third approach is to brainstorm with children about acceptable expressions. When I did this with my class of two- and three-year-olds, we made a hysterical list of forty-eight expletives, none of which was a "bad" word. My top three picks were "Fiddlesticks," "Good gravy," and "Wowzer!"

READING TIP:
Elbert's Bad Word by Audrey Wood. Ages two and up. Elbert uses a word he overhears and later learns some more suitable replacements.

Do you want a spanking?

If spanking is part of your parenting repertoire—and hopefully it isn't—why confuse the issue by asking a child about it? You'll never get a positive response to this question! If children learn to behave well because they fear physical punishment, the point has been lost, the message tainted. As the well-known and well-loved pediatrician Dr. T. Berry Brazelton says, "Corporal punishment is no longer acceptable in a world of continuing violence." You can teach children that you mean what you say without using swats and slaps.

Children most often act out when they are tired, anxious, or overwhelmed. When people say, "She's just doing that for the attention," they're probably right. She likely needs your help in navigating whatever the situation is. The solution is to stay attuned to the child and, whenever possible, give her the attention and guidance she needs *before* the negative behavior erupts. When you want to stop certain behavior, calmly intervene. Try repeating what you want, or use a firmer tone, or even physically remove the child from the situation. If you do, state the limit firmly: "You are not allowed to kick your sister, so I am moving you away from her to keep everyone safe." Sometimes children aren't ready to play together unattended.

You can have dessert after you clean your plate.

There are more nutrition books on the market than anyone could count, and not one says that children should clean their plates. Young boys and girls naturally eat when they are hungry and stop when they are full. Eating bargains with a child bring an atmosphere of control to the dinner table. Child development expert Penelope Leach has a better plan for feeding children called the "division of responsibility." The grown-up is responsible for preparing and presenting the food, and the child is responsible for what and how much, and even *whether*, he eats. Most children up to age three will ultimately eat a healthy diet (though not necessarily all in one day) if given lean protein, fresh vegetables, whole grains, and fruit. Don't fret if a child goes through the typical phase of objecting to lots of foods—keep offering them. Kids tend to have short memories about their dislikes.

Using sweet desserts as a bribe elevates sugar, with its already desirable taste (and bad effects on growing bodies), to an even higher level of attractiveness. There's no rule that desserts should even be on a daily menu, and that they be rich and sweet. Consider providing only an occasional dessert or make it fresh fruit. Talking about what a child does or doesn't eat is unnecessary—in fact, never mentioning it is the best approach (though not easy for some of us).

Reading Tip:

Gregory The Terrible Eater by Mitchell Sharmat. Ages two and up. Gregory the goat learns to like eating just about anything.

I'll give you something special if you pick up your toys.

A child cannot be forced to do something. Simply ask for the action you want without bribing, bargaining, or begging—or ask him to do it along with you. If he refuses, you can set an example by cleaning up the toys yourself and tell him how you feel: "I asked you to clean up and you didn't. So I'm doing it instead. Next time you can do it." The child will likely cooperate eventually. Most young children want to be helpful and will take pride in their accomplishments—even housekeeping. If messes are overwhelming, reduce the number of toys available (a toy rotation works well), and create an environment primed for success.

I'm going to leave without you.

Never quite sure if Mom or Dad really meant it, I remember waiting until they were fully out of the toy store before deciding I'd better join them. The store sure was fun, but I didn't want to spend the night there! Many parents use the threat of leaving because it is so effective. It evokes fear of abandonment, which motivates children to comply. But at what cost? This type of threat damages child–parent trust. Also, at some point a child will figure out that you won't really leave her behind, and then this ploy no longer works. Instead of a threat, interact in a more straightforward manner: "It's time to leave now. Let's hold hands and walk out together, or I can carry you." Treat children respectfully, even when they don't get what they want. After one or two tests, they will have learned to take you at your word.

Reading Tips:

Corduroy by Don Freeman. Ages two and up. A loveable bear gets lost in a department store.

Stellaluna by Janell Cannon. Ages two and up. This plucky fruit bat is separated from and then reunited with his worried mom.

"If you eat that ice cream nicely, I'll buy you a toy."

Just wait till your father gets home.

Don't pass the buck! It undermines your authority. If you are in charge when a child misbehaves, you are in charge of addressing the issue. In reality, it is comforting to children to know that the adult taking care of them is responsible for setting and enforcing limits. When you don't put restraints on a child's behavior, this can be frightening. He might act thrilled to be getting away with something, but in his mind there is a subconscious question: *How will I stay safe if there's nothing holding me back?*

A young child has a short attention span, which makes delayed enforcement confusing. Give immediate feedback with narration and a clear consequence: "You will not play with trucks for the rest of the day because you threw a truck at your sister. She is crying and has a bruise on her head." He will understand that the consequence was for what just happened.

READING TIP:

David Gets in Trouble by David Shannon. Ages one and up. David gets into everything and is also very loved.

See if you ever get another toy.

This is an empty threat—you know it, and so does the child. Instead of saying this, share your feelings about him treating his property with disrespect, and state the consequences. Say, for example, "John, you left your nice pens lying around with the tops off. They dry out quickly if you don't take care of them. If you leave the tops off again, I'm going to put them away for two days." Also, you can let kids in on the fact that toys, videos, and art supplies cost money—money you are doubtless willing to spend if he is appreciative and treats his things well.

READING TIP:

My Friend and I by Lisa Jahn-Clough. Ages two and up. Two friends have trouble sharing and some toys get broken in the process. Then they make up and fix them together.

6 How Are You Feeling?
Handling emotions

Expressing feelings comes naturally for young children—it is their first fluent language. During babyhood they communicated with crying, laughter, murmurs, and all sorts of other specific sounds. As parents got accustomed to baby's wails and whimpers they said things like, "That's his hungry cry," or "She's just fussing because she's bored." This basic "baby language" is universal. It serves infants for a while, and then they add gestures and words to express themselves.

But knowing one's feelings and expressing them verbally is a slow and complex process. As children gain language, they need gentle guidance and reminders to "use your words." Sometimes young children fall back on crying and physical acting out to express emotions they can't yet verbalize. Instead of disciplining them, adults can help children learn to effectively express themselves. For example, "Yes, Scott took your toy and you seem very angry. But you can respond without hitting. Tell him how you feel when he takes something you were playing with, and use words to ask for it back." Talk to the offending child: "Scott, Malcolm is upset. He's trying to tell you how he feels about what you did with his toy. You both seem frustrated because we only have one of these trucks." Then ask the kids how they might resolve the situation. Nine times out of ten they will come up with a solution that works for them—often one you wouldn't have imagined.

The intense emotional lives of children can be challenging—in fact, sometimes it drives us nuts. An adult's first reaction to a child's moodiness or strong outbursts is often an attempt to moderate them. Without considering the impact of our own words, we encourage children to push aside what they are feeling, or to question the validity of their reactions. How often have you said, "Oh, it's not so bad"? Such well-meaning comments set the stage for children to start ignoring or hiding their feelings. Rather than discount their emotional states, help young children learn to pay attention to them, and to express themselves in acceptable ways. After an upsetting experience, describe what occurred before dealing with the practicalities: "You didn't want to have your diaper changed, and now you're crying."

Negative outbursts in young children tend to be more intense when their basic needs are not met. This is a natural form of self-care. (Try to run errands when everyone is well rested and take along a snack.) The frustration a child feels about not getting what she wants, sometimes compounded by not being able to communicate it well, is demonstrated most spectacularly in temper tantrums. Parents, teachers, and caregivers alike have to weather these storms from time to time. Get the child to a safe place if needed (an uncluttered carpeted area works well), and allow her to fully let off steam. Keep what you say simple, and acknowledge the child's feelings with something like, "You are so mad and frustrated right now."

Most children outgrow the tantrum phase as their verbal skills increase. For this reason, few children throw tantrums past age four. If an older child has prolonged outbursts on a grand scale, consider the possibility that you are being manipulated. If you remain calm and don't give in, tantrums that are used to control others will gradually cease.

When a child's behavior triggers a strong negative feeling in you, try to temper your reaction. Yelling and stamping your feet in frustration is not the behavior you want to model. Use clear statements to help kids understand how they impact others: "When you hit me, I feel frustrated and angry. Stop now." This two-part statement, "When you … I feel …" encompasses both sides: the child did something, and the adult had a reaction to it. Neither side changes their feelings, but both can be accountable for how these feelings are expressed. Giving children examples of an authentic and appropriate emotional expression is a good way to teach them. Years ago, I had a surprising experience that demonstrated the value of this.

On my way to work at a child care center, I was verbally assaulted by an obviously unstable woman. Stunned, I walked into the classroom and pulled my supervisor aside to tell her what had happened. As I did, tears spilled out. I felt inclined to leave, fearing that the two-and-a-half-year-olds would worry about me. My wise mentor suggested that I stay instead and talk with them about the incident. I did. What followed was a touching interaction as this group of often unruly and self-focused children snuggled close, patted me on the back, and asked, "Why did she say mean things to you, Sarah?" Minutes later I felt much better and thanked everyone for listening. I was surprised that these very young children could empathize when I shared my upset with them. Not suppressing feelings with kids and talking about difficult experiences can reap unexpected rewards.

Hearing these doesn't feel so good

There's nothing to be afraid of.

Trying to talk children out of fears can hinder their natural responses to a sometimes unsafe world. If you turn on the evening news—something you might do every day in front of your children—it's clear there are plenty of things to be afraid of. Denying this to a young child can multiply her fears rather than reduce them. Many of us remember the common and very real childhood fear of the dark. Some practical ways to alleviate this stress are to leave the bedroom door ajar or install a night light. One smart mom I know helped her three-year-old make a sign for the bedroom door that read *No Goblins Allowed. Ka-Poof!* Help children to be brave and navigate their fears by asking about them, offering validation, and brainstorming solutions.

Anxiety about an upcoming event should be addressed. What might seem routine to adults can be scary to children. Some children will stay calmer with more lead time, while for others it causes unneeded worry.

Pay attention to how a child responds when given forewarning and act accordingly. For example, some kids panic if told in the morning about an afternoon medical appointment. If the child has a toy doctor's kit, she can become familiar with the tools and procedures. Taking along a stuffed animal for the doctor to "check out" can also soothe an anxious little boy or girl. Speak positively and remind the child that visiting a doctor is something everyone does: "You're going to the doctor just like I do. Doctors help keep our bodies healthy and strong." Instead of discounting fears, offer support.

READING TIPS:

Felix Feels Better by Rosemary Wells. Ages one and up. Felix's doctor really does help him out.

There's a Nightmare in My Closet by Mercer Mayer. Ages three and up. A little boy discovers that his nightmare isn't so scary after all.

Wemberly Worried by Kevin Henkes. Ages three and up. Wemberly worries so much, but making a friend at school really helps.

The Dark by Robert Munsch. Ages three and up. Jule Ann uses quick thinking to capture the dark.

Stop crying right this minute.

Because crying is a natural and necessary form of release, it makes no sense to tell a child not to do it. A crying jag can be due to physical as well as emotional stress—or a desire to manipulate. Does your toddler lose it every afternoon at 4:00? Maybe he can't wait until dinner and needs a snack. Does Molly break down as soon as she gets home from school? Ask her teachers for input, but consider the possibility that her crying is not related to school. Maybe she has figured out that if she fusses after school, you will let her watch TV.

When crying escalates to loud screams, tell a child that you need distance from his volume. Reassure him with an offer of comfort when he has quieted down. Use clear language that defines boundaries and does not belittle his passionate feelings: "I know you're upset that you lost your stuffed kitten today, but we are not going to get a new one.

You can be sad as long as you need. Crying might help you feel better and that's fine, but screaming hurts my ears. I'm going to move away a bit and cover my ears. When you're not so loud, I'll be available."

READING TIPS:

Why Do You Cry? Not a Sob Story by Kate Klise. Ages three and up. Little Rabbit vows to never cry again but then finds out that crying is just part of life.

Knuffle Bunny: A Cautionary Tale by Mo Willems. Ages one and up. Trixie tries to tell her dad she's lost her stuffed animal, but she doesn't know any words!

Sticks and stones may break my bones, but names will never hurt me.

The first time a grown-up quoted this common nursery saying to me, I was so offended! My feelings had been hurt by a child's teasing and name calling, and, as we all know, that does indeed hurt. Even as adults we are often hurt by words. This indirect way of telling a child to deny painful feelings is insensitive. Of course, it's faster and easier than talking to a child about feelings. But that is worthwhile: "You seem very upset that Karen called you those mean names." Or you might ask, "What do you think about what she said? Do you think it's true?"

Getting involved in conflict resolution between two kids is time-consuming and not always necessary. Instead, ask the child who complains about being called a name to go tell the name-caller how he feels. Be a good model for communication skills by addressing the issue and offering to follow up afterwards: "Sounds like you are mad about what Nick said to you. Why don't you go talk with him about it? Come back and tell me how it went."

READING TIPS:

Words Are Not for Hurting by Elizabeth Verdick. Ages two and up. Words are very useful but can sometimes be hurtful.

Best Best Friends by Margaret Chodos-Irvine. Ages two and up. A story about the ups and downs of friendship.

You're always so grumpy.

Calling attention to a child's bad moods—whether we complain or act like it's "cute"—is not helpful. All of us, including children, are cranky at times. Adults can ignore irritability or address it directly. I often ask, "How are things not going your way today?" This open-ended question allows for a dialogue between you and the child. Perhaps you will learn something important about the child's emotional or physical well-being. If she is simply in an off mood—perhaps mirroring your mood?—there's no reason to harp on it. The last thing I want pointed out when I'm feeling grumpy is just that.

If a dark cloud has descended, try to pull back and recall recent events. Acknowledge any disruptions or difficulties you are aware of: "It sure has been a tough week! We've been so busy, and going to Grandma's on Saturday wore everyone out." This helps a child to not feel isolated.

READING TIP:

Today I Feel Silly: & Other Moods That Make my Day by Jamie Lee Curtis. Ages two and up. This child has good days and not-so-good days and that's okay.

Don't be shy.

In one way or another, every child is shy about something. This usually varies with the setting. It is unwise to push a child to be outgoing—his shyness helps him manage his level of comfort in different circumstances. Give a child time to adjust to new situations and people. When talking to him about his hesitancy, use descriptive words like *cautious* and *observant,* Or say, "You are not saying hello to our guest. Are you deciding how you feel?" If you want the child to say "Hello," make a direct request instead of telling him to discount what he feels. When a child is holding back, you can address the adult in question with a simple comment about him still warming up to the situation, then move on with the conversation. It's best not to speak *about* the child ("Andrew is just shy"). This is inconsiderate and places a limiting label on him.

Sometimes a child's hesitancy is not so much shyness as a feeling of mistrust. You can teach children to respect others while still maintaining good personal boundaries. This means allowing a little one to trust his intuition—let him decide for himself whether or not to give Daddy's best friend a hug.

READING TIPS:

Shy Charles by Rosemary Wells. Ages three and up. Charles might be shy, but he still manages to save the day.

Shrinking Violet by Cari Best. Ages three and up. Violet's wise teacher finds a role in the school play tailored to her shy temperament.

The Story of Ferdinand by Munro Leaf. Ages two and up. A young bull who is shy at heart inadvertently ends up in the bullfighting ring.

There's no reason to be upset.

Children feel their emotions very intensely, and this is not a bad thing. Once a child has felt something to its very depth, she is freer to let it go and move on. In talking to an upset child, focus on her feelings and try to redirect her attention: "You sure are mad about your tower falling over. I really understand. Maybe it was demolition time for that building? Try being the dump truck that carries away the rubble." Or offer to hold the child until she has calmed herself.

Dealing with upsets varies with the situation. If you are at a restaurant and Joe is furiously screaming because his crayon broke, remind him that, although it is understandable he is upset, he may not yell and disturb everyone else. This would be a great time to try distracting him with a silly song. Sometimes follow-through is more important. If this means abandoning your meal midstream, so be it. On occasion it's necessary to accept evidence that a child is not yet ready to sit through a restaurant meal.

READING TIP:

When Sophie Gets Angry—Really, Really Angry by Molly Bang. Ages one and up. Sophie needs to work through her feelings.

"There's no reason to be afraid of the dark."

I am not crying—everything is just fine.

Young children need not be shielded from all negative and upsetting feelings that adults have. In fact, if you want kids to talk about *their* feelings, talking about your own is a teaching opportunity. Demonstrate to kids how you would like them to express painful or strong emotions. Be straightforward: "I am sad about Grandma being sick. I know you don't often see me cry, but it helps me feel better when I'm upset." If a child seems worried, offer reassurance: "It's not your fault I'm crying, and you don't have to do anything to fix my sadness. I'll feel better in a little while."

READING TIP:

The Feelings Book by Todd Parr. Ages two and up. No feelings are wrong and there are many ways to express them.

You're making me so mad.

This statement confuses a child by implying that he or she is in charge of your emotions. A child's behavior might trigger strong reactions in us, but that doesn't make the child responsible for them. While the emotional impact goes both ways, we alone are accountable for our reactions. Respond with a "When you ... I feel ..." statement: "When you scream so loudly, I feel angry." Or use redirection: "I am a small little mouse and I can't hear you unless you are very, very quiet. Squeak, squeak, what did you say?"

A similar comment about a child's effect on you is, "You're giving me a headache." A difficult interaction with a child could certainly contribute to a tension headache, but blaming the child for it only worsens the situation. Hearing this kind of statement, a child might think she is responsible for how you feel and then worry about it.

7 | What a Shame!
The inner critic

Shame is excruciating for children. It causes them to feel cut off, flawed, and just plain awful. The shamed child often develops an inner critic who makes it difficult to feel good or do anything right. This can also cause serious adjustment problems in adulthood. But to talk about our shame is, well, shameful, so the feeling is largely ignored. We need to understand how this vitally important emotion functions because it can both hinder and help children.

We don't want children to believe they are irrevocably bad, but allowing them to feel ashamed about undesirable behavior can motivate change. John Bradshaw, in *Healing the Shame That Binds You,* divides shame into "toxic" and "healthy" forms. Healthy shame comes from within and lets us know we are human, that we do make mistakes and that our capabilities are limited. A child might feel ashamed of an action (she broke something) or an inaction (she didn't stick up for a friend). Human beings are naturally designed for these kinds of feelings, the self-monitoring that goes with a conscience. With children, of course, it takes time for this conscience to develop!

Toxic shame, on the other hand, causes a child to feel like he is a mistake, a situation he'll never be able to change. Your reaction to a misdeed can cause toxic shame if you are condemning. A child feels faulty and devalued when an adult says, "I can't believe you took this and broke it, and then didn't even tell me!" Healthy shame can be promoted by a calm response that acknowledges what a child is probably feeling: "I see you took this from the cupboard without asking, and then you broke it.

You must be feeling pretty bad about that since you hid it." You can also express how you feel: "I am sad it's broken, even if it was an accident." But try to let children learn from their *own* feelings, not yours.

Part of growing up is learning what behaviors are acceptable, so giving kids appropriate feedback is crucial. Make sure a child hears unmistakably that it is his *behavior* that's unacceptable, not he himself. If Sean is berated and called a slob because he doesn't keep his room clean, he may store the "slob" message and be hindered by it later. Toxic shame can result from this kind of stigma, and also from humiliation, embarrassment, or ridicule. Sometimes adults make fun of children's looks, habits, brainpower, or skills. Even when they offer the lame excuse, "I was just teasing," this is always detrimental.

Children's negative behavior can provide valuable clues to their inner development. Lying, stealing, hiding broken objects, bathroom accidents, and especially sexual behavior in children can provoke strong adult reactions, likely because we ourselves were once ashamed of the same things. Take note of your personal triggers—perhaps jotting down your feelings and revisiting them later when you have time to reflect on your early life. Doing this before talking to a child about his actions will help you respond in a more supportive, loving manner.

In Dorothy Law Nolte's very popular poem *Children Learn What They Live,* two lines express the guiding principle well: "If children live with criticism, they learn to condemn," and "If children live with acceptance, they learn to love." By not causing shame through criticism and ridicule, and letting the kids in our lives experience more acceptance and honesty, we can give them a healthy emotional start.

Words no child wants to hear

I can't believe you did that!

Young kids always keep us on our toes because, as fairly new human beings, they have quite a lot of learning to do. Toddlers will assault others, ruin property, abuse a pet, or put themselves in danger. Instead of making a hurtful statement, just describe what you see.

At times a child's actions *can* be shocking, particularly when issues of morality come into play. If a four-year-old steals something, she might not know that this is wrong. By staying low-key and not scolding, you give a child the opportunity to think about her action, even if she did know better. Instead of erupting in outrage, simply address the misdeed directly: "Georgia, this toy does not belong to you. I know you took it from the store. We have to return it because taking something that doesn't belong to you is wrong. Those toys are for sale, and you have to pay money for them before bringing them home." Don't embarrass her at the store by insisting that she make a big, formal apology. Healthy shame should keep the child from trying this behavior again.

READING TIPS:

Alexander and the Terrible, Horrible, No Good, Very Bad Day by Judith Viorst. Ages three and up. Trouble follows Alexander all day, but his mom understands that sometimes that happens.

It Wasn't Me by Udo Weigelt. Ferret works hard to collect some berries and when they turn up missing, Raven is accused of stealing them. The real culprit is a surprise.

I'm so disappointed in you.

How often have you heard this classic? The sentiment is genuine, but it can cause a child to believe *he* is the disappointment rather than his behavior. Instead of focusing on how let down you are, try talking about the situation: "You're not following directions, so now we will leave." Or to a toddler you might say, "You are not listening. I asked you twice to climb down from there. Now I will help by lifting you down." Maintaining a neutral tone and a "poker face" can keep a child from having a blow-up when you reinforce a limit.

As children get older, it might seem like disappointing behavior is increasing because your expectations have grown. There is still nothing to be gained by a big negative reaction. Try to address a misdeed unemotionally: "Sheila, I heard from your teacher that you were bullying a child at school today." Don't freak out if she denies it, and listen to her side of the story. State how you feel and ask questions: "I'm upset to hear that you took Janet's snack and called her names. Can you tell me more about what happened?" Discuss the child's actions and encourage empathy: "How would you feel if someone called you names?"

READING TIP:

Horton Hatches the Egg by Dr. Seuss. Ages two and up. An elephant and a bird shed light on responsibility, both the hard work and its rewards.

Who do you think you are?

This insulting question pops out all too often when adults feel disrespected and want to be seen as top dog. If we feel indignant or out of control, our tone gets snippy and that only escalates the situation. Instead of using words that belittle a child, tell him how you feel and what you want from him: "I don't like the way you're talking to me. Please change your tone of voice and tell me what you want in a different way." If emotions are running high and communication isn't happening, suggest taking a break to calm down. These options defuse the interaction and give him a chance to think about his behavior. It also teaches a child about respect from an early age. By showing respect for him you are guiding him in how to be respectful of you and others.

You just never learn.

This phrase reminds me of the father in a great movie, *Muriel's Wedding,* who has a habit of describing all of his children as "useless." The main character has taken her dad's shaming assessment to heart, but she eventually changes the way she sees herself—and changes her life for the better. If you give a child a limiting judgment as a starting off place, it puts her at a huge disadvantage. These are words that sting and can hinder emotional and intellectual growth.

If a child is failing to learn a new skill or task, reassess your expectations. Talk to her about a repetitive mistake or omission she may be making: "I notice that every time you get undressed you leave your clothes on the floor. What do you think would help you to put them in the hamper?" This fosters learning and growth rather than shame and defeat. "You can do it" and "Keep practicing" are ways to speak encouragingly to a child whose efforts have not been successful thus far. Have realistic expectations, keeping personality and temperament in mind, and give her time.

READING TIP:

Edwardo: The Horriblest Boy in the Whole Wide World. Ages two and up. Edwardo behaves exactly as everyone expects him to, for better and for worse.

Why can't you be more like your brother?

The answer to this common question is easier than most adults think: your child is busy being himself! Siblings are competitive enough without Mom or Dad adding fuel to this already crackling fire by comparing them. Children in the same family are highly unlikely to have the same personalities, talents, and preferences. In fact, most parents marvel at the differences between their kids. You can give a child feedback that doesn't shame him and still acknowledges his individuality: "Jon, I know you often get aggravated in crowded situations, but we have one more stop to make before we leave the mall." Or try redirecting his attention, for example, "Let's sing a song on our way to the next store."

Reading Tips:

I Love You the Purplest by Barbara M Joosse. Ages two and up. This mom tells each of her boys how different they are from each other, and how wonderful each is.

You're All My Favorites by Sam McBratney. Ages two and up. A father reassures his three children they are all loved individually.

Shame on you!

This most basic statement for evoking humiliation is simply punitive. The child ends up feeling bad about himself instead of learning, which should be the goal of discipline. When a child has made a poor choice, try to focus on the behavior rather than the child and give feedback on what to do or not do *next time*. Be clear with young children about what you want changed, addressing the conduct itself: "You took gum from my purse without asking. This purse is mine, and I don't want you to have gum without my permission. Next time you need to ask me first." Then perhaps add a "gum restriction" as a consequence and talk about what happened: "I have told you not to take my things without asking and I'm frustrated that you haven't listened."

It can be particularly difficult to say the right thing when children are cruel to animals or to one another. When a child has hurt a younger one or is intentionally destructive, those three little words want to come out. We think they should know better, and it may be true, but this reaction condemns rather than teaches. Instead, use a severe tone to get attention and respond to what happened: "You hit your baby sister. That hurts her and is not okay. No hitting!" And share your feelings about it: "I feel angry and scared when you hit your sister. I don't like that."

8 | Everybody Has a Body

Keeping the messages clear

American culture is loaded with hang-ups about bodies—how they look, what we put in them, and their sexual functions. These often warped messages produce untold numbers of mixed up and unhappy adults whose feelings influence children. What parents and caregivers say to young children about looks and food and sex is vitally important. Just as kids need help with emotional and intellectual growth, they also need guidance in developing a healthy attitude toward their bodies. The process starts with newborns as they learn about anatomy by exploring all their own fascinating parts. As children grow, they gather important messages from the adults in their lives and from the larger world.

Mirror, Mirror on the Wall

Our social environment is obsessed with looks—we are constantly bombarded with media images of "preferred" facial and body types. Unless kids grow up in total isolation, they soon learn which types to aspire to. They also pay attention to how adults talk about appearance, including their own. Do you say things like, "She's big as a cow," "It's too bad about his nose," or "I hate my thighs"? Children tend to mimic not only your language but your attitude—comments like these imply that putting down others and one's self is normal and accepted.

Talking to a child about his appearance can be a minefield. Many youngsters are overly concerned about how they look, so if you do mention a child's looks, don't overdo it. Occasionally commenting on a child's special features is fine: "You have such beautiful shiny hair" or,

"I see those bright blue eyes." But rather than emphasize appearance, appreciate and acknowledge a child's special talents and interests as well. Something such as, "You run so fast! What strong legs you have."

Children and Food

As kids develop their relationships with food, adults are key players—grocery shoppers, cooks, and role models. With the alarming rise in obesity and Type 2 diabetes among children, parents and caregivers need to seriously consider their part in these sad health trends. Do we pay lip service to the idea of healthy food but take the family to fast-food places several times a week? Young children who get whatever they want to eat are primed for not only gaining excess weight but other health problems down the road. Parents need to be in charge of what foods are ordered in restaurants and what is offered at home.

The adults in a child's life can do a lot to offset poor eating habits and influences. Besides taking obvious steps like preparing healthy, well balanced meals, we can educate ourselves on nutrition and talk to kids about it. For example, "These beans have lots of protein, which helps your body grow." "We don't buy that snack because it has something called trans fat that is bad for our bodies." Even young children can be interested in how various kinds of food affect the growth of their bodies.

Private Parts

The first principle in talking to children about body parts and their functions—though awkward for some of us—is using anatomically correct language. While many adults use the common terms for elimination, "pee" and "poop," euphemisms for private parts should be avoided. What kind of feelings does a child have about his genitals if they are kept shrouded in mystery or made to seem dirty? Boys have not only a penis, but a foreskin (sometimes), testicles, and scrotum. Girls have a vulva, labia, a clitoris, and a vagina. As a teacher, I heard the inevitable discussion during bathroom breaks about who was using the "right" term. I learned to keep a straight face while explaining to young ones that "weenie" and "pecker" are words that people sometimes use instead of *penis,* the correct term. Along with the proper words, youngsters should learn how to wash and wipe their own private areas as soon as they are able.

Adults can easily sabotage a child's positive connection to his sexual self with their own discomfort. Try to respond calmly to a child's very normal sexual curiosity rather than evoke shame by acting shocked. Doctors Mary Calderone and James Ramey, in *Talking With Your Child About Sex,* offer some sound insight: "Deliberate adult avoidance of the area between the waist and the knees can hardly go unnoticed by the child, especially when other body parts are freely mentioned. Since the child already knows that this is an important pleasure center of the body, such avoidance can cause confusion and lay the groundwork for later problems." If you are confused about how to talk with kids about sexuality, reproduction, and self-protection, there are many good books on these topics.

Another advantage for children who are comfortable with their bodies and know the correct terms is they are less likely to be sexually abused. This knowledge empowers them with a sense of ownership over their bodies. Encourage kids to stand up for themselves by saying "No!" in any situation that makes them anxious. A pushover child is an easy target for exploitation. Since children are more likely to be molested by someone they know, make sure that kids understand that they don't have to do something just because a grown-up—even a family friend— or an older child says so. Teach a child who feels uncomfortable about a situation to say, "That part of my body is private" or simply, "Don't touch me." A guideline children can understand is that the body parts their bathing suits cover are restricted areas, to be touched only by the child and certain other people. Even those people—parents, caregivers, and doctors—should honor a child's feelings about being touched. Adults with their rules, habits, and issues greatly impact a child's feelings about his sexuality—and about his looks and food. Pay attention to the messages you send.

Is this how to say it?

That didn't hurt.

Adults typically say this to stave off crying after a child gets an injection or has a minor mishap. Toddlers and preschoolers often react to a bonk or scratch with buckets of tears, sometimes more out of frustration than pain. Maybe the child just needs some attention, a little rub or a kiss for that hurt. Ultimately, a child should be the authority on his body—sometimes seemingly minor mishaps can result in serious injury. If a child continues to complain of pain, consider seeking medical attention.

Describing a situation and asking questions are ways of responding that don't minimize what happened: "You hit your head on that bar. Does it hurt? Where?" You can also offer comforting reassurance: "It's a very small bump. I think you will be okay." Let young children know that their bodies are smart and capable of healing—they can feel betrayed when they are hurt or ill. When there's a small injury, you can say, "Your body knows what to do—it's already working to heal that scrape." Preschool children are often fascinated to learn the big words and facts associated with healing. For a cut, you can introduce words like *coagulate* and *platelets*. A child's interest in these processes can distract from the pain he or she might be experiencing.

READING TIP:
Rachel Fister's Blister by Amy MacDonald. Ages six months and up. The whole town gathers to try to fix Rachel's annoying blister.

Don't talk to strangers.

This blanket statement might well cause more problems than it solves. "Stranger danger" should not be where adults conclude the matter of a child's personal safety, especially since strangers are not the most likely to cause harm to children. But do warn children to not go *anywhere* with a stranger—even if offered a treat or a peek at some puppies, or approached about help or some type of emergency. Teach young kids to keep personal information to themselves, to never accept a gift from someone they don't know, and to walk away from anyone who makes them uncomfortable, perhaps saying something like, "I'm going back over to my dad." On the other hand, children should learn how to recognize and approach a helping person they don't know if they become lost or need assistance—for example, a woman with children or a cashier at a store.

It is important to help children stay tuned in to their feelings about the people in their lives. This means everyone from Uncle Albert to the strangers they meet at playgrounds and other public places. These are usually pleasant interactions, but if you or a child has an unsettling experience in a setting like this, discuss it: "Today at the park that man with the dog asked me a lot of questions. What did you think of him?" Give kids a chance to observe and think; this will serve them better than scare tactics. The best self-protection skill you can foster in children is the ability to trust their instincts and act on them.

READING TIP:
   It's My Body by Lory Freeman. Ages one and up. A child learns that her body is hers and that she is in charge of it.

Stop that or you'll hurt yourself.

This statement isn't necessarily true but a child can unconsciously fulfill the prophecy—so it just might be! Instead of implying that the child is making a dangerous choice, acknowledge that you are scared and make a request: "I feel afraid when I see you up there. Please get down." Another approach is to use inquiry and reflection. Ask a child to reflect on her actions or whereabouts: "Tania, how far out on that tree limb do you think it's safe to go? Will that branch still hold you if you go out farther?" By asking Tania to stop and think, yet not telling her what to do, she is given the opportunity to take a safer course on her own. Children gain a more realistic understanding of their bodies when empowered to assess some risks themselves.

"I fixed your favorite low-carb snack."

You're looking a little chubby.

Calling attention to a child's weight can be dangerous territory in our image-obsessed culture. Today's alarming rate of eating disorders is fueled by the messages that children see and hear everywhere about acceptable body types. Rather than ignore this fact, let them know that people's body types differ; some will be stocky, others slender, even when consuming similar diets. When it comes to Barbie dolls, you could point out that real people don't look like that ... unless they have some ribs cut out!

Instead of making a negative comment about a child's weight, just say nothing. The child is not at fault and body size cannot be altered quickly. Dietary changes must start with the adults who buy and prepare the child's food. Let youngsters sometimes be included in the shopping and food preparation, and give explanations about nutrition, weight, and exercise. Saying something helpful or practical is better than a tactless remark.

READING TIPS:

You Look Ridiculous Said the Rhinoceros to the Hippopotamus by Bernard Waber. Ages two and up. The hippo tries to be something he's not but ends up loving who he is.

I Like Me! by Nancy Carlson. Ages one and up. Everyone should like himself.

The stork brought us a baby.

Perhaps the babies in your family came from the cabbage patch? There are some imaginative sayings about where babies come from, but why lie? If a child doesn't ask, you are under no obligation to tell. But if he or she does, you could say, "Our baby came out of my uterus [or womb], a special part of the body that protected baby while he grew." If she asks how the baby gets out, you can explain that too. Most experts agree that providing only the information requested is the least overwhelming for children.

For those who want to know the how in addition to the where, start with a simple explanation like, "A sperm from Daddy and an egg from Mommy came together to make the baby." This common explanation tends to cause confusion: "Our baby grew from a seed in Mommy's stomach." Children are so literal they might fear getting pregnant from swallowing a grape seed! Anatomically correct words are always best.

READING TIPS:

Where Willy Went by Nicholas Allan. Ages two and up. A sperm takes a journey and helps make a person.

Where Did I Come From? by Peter Mayle. Ages six and up. This straightforward text tells all the facts.

You're such a klutz.

If this has ever been said to you, you know how it feels—awful. And the more you focus on the feeling, the klutzier you become. The same is true with children. Their bodies, emotions, and intellect go through an eighteen-year period of rapid development and change. All kids experience stages when they are ungainly and uncoordinated. Pointing this out only increases a child's self-consciousness. To counter a child's physical embarrassments, emphasize the strides she is making: "You tripped during part of the obstacle course, but then you crossed the balance beam at the end without falling off once." Or don't say anything at all. Much like the stutter of some young kids, if you ignore clumsiness, it will usually resolve itself.

READING TIP:

The Very Clumsy Click Beetle by Eric Carle. Ages one and up. The beetle tries and tries and finally achieves his goal.

Stay still!

Many of us assume that if a child is moving around, he is not listening. This is not true. Some children actually learn *best* when moving or doodling. A child's ability to focus and sit still is heavily influenced by his or her temperament and learning style. Classroom teachers rely on children who have a calm temperament and will sit still and listen up. Children with physical learning styles are often discouraged from being that way and may even be misdiagnosed with attention deficit disorder. If a child's foot is tapping as he paints a picture, let it be—it may be helping him concentrate.

Of course sometimes we do need for a child to hold still. If a toddler's movement is interfering with an activity (getting her dressed, for example), explain what you want: "I can't help you get your shirt on while you are waving your arms. Please work with me to get you dressed.

Then we can play." Or engage the child's imagination by pretending the wayward arms are something else: "Slither that snake into the hole." Engaging a child's imagination usually helps, and it can lighten your mood, too.

Don't touch yourself down there.

There is no justification for saying this—it's natural for young children to explore their bodies and "check out" the private parts of their anatomy. Telling children to not touch themselves in certain places can send the message that they shouldn't be comfortable with all parts of their bodies, or that these areas are shameful. Children might also take this or a similar admonition literally and become anxious about necessary touching for using the toilet or washing. When toddlers first discover these usually covered parts, name them just as you do the other body parts. Say "That's your penis" the same as you would "That's your nose."

Exploration may lead to genital stimulation and the pleasurable feelings it produces. Never scold the child, but try offering another activity as distraction. For parents, often the most effective distraction is increased attention and affection.

9 | The Power Paradox
It's not about control

Young kids are essentially powerless. Their rights are few and their capabilities limited, making the parent–child relationship significantly unequal. The size difference only accentuates this. Lack of language ability and limited vocabulary are also contributing factors. Babies and toddlers see their parents as gods, but in the next few years this viewpoint starts to fade. Use your short time as a deity in a benevolent way!

A Balancing Act

Children gradually gain power as they grow to adulthood, a process that takes most of us about twenty years. Early childhood in particular is full of strife. Once a child is not a baby anymore, he magically forms his own opinions and asserts his individuality and newfound power through actions and words. Adults typically feel challenged by this and react by trying to control the child. We say things like, "Don't talk to me like that," or "You stop that right now!" These responses only fuel the fire and lead to power struggles. And we often feel bad after those whether we lose *or* win.

To feel secure, little ones actually want to know there are limits. Imagine yourself driving across a high bridge with no railings—it would be scary. Assuming there are guardrails, we don't crash against them to test their strength, but small children do the equivalent of this. They will check out a restraint, perhaps banging on a baby gate to see whether it holds. Kids also test verbal limits. Toddlers in particular need to know, *Does she really mean it?*

Young children typically regard limits as circumstantial. If you tell a small child "no hitting" when she hits a friend, she doesn't understand this as a universal rule. You'll need to say it again when she wallops the cat. And even if she understands not to use potty talk at home, it may not carry over to preschool. So when a little one tests various situations, don't assume that she is just being obstinate. Because limits need continued reinforcement, it is wise not to set too many—and to establish good childproofing. Putting a barricade in front of the fireplace or keeping your pocketbook out of reach eliminates the need to make rules about these off-limits things. If kids have less to push up against, they will push less. This is the paradox of power. Children grow and learn best in the least restrictive yet safe environment we can provide.

Kid Power

Just as children need limits, they want and need to experience personal power. This means the feeling of being able to take action, to know that one's words will be listened to and one's individuality acknowledged. A child will feel powerful when he learns new skills such as walking and talking. The sense of achievement is written all over his grinning face when he triumphantly toddles across the room without your help. While we might assist a child in learning to walk, the success comes through his own effort.

It's very important that a child's natural can-do attitude is not thwarted in the early years. Allowing kids to make and then correct mistakes is empowering for them. But it can be hard for grown-ups to watch the try-fail-persevere-succeed cycle. A little frustration can motivate a child, although parents and caregivers should not be hands-off when kids are in an unsafe situation, or are very upset. Talk to a little one about her efforts: "You keep trying to get up that climbing wall even though you've slipped three times. You'll get the hang of it soon." If frustration is mounting, you can offer to help, but always ask first and respect a "no" answer if you get one.

Young children have little power over their lives, but that doesn't mean they don't want it! It can be annoying to always have grown-ups telling you what to do, and when and how to do it. Think of ways to give kids some choice in their daily lives. For example, let your toddler choose (from a pre-selected assortment of clothes) what he will wear. The empowerment that comes from having a choice can also be incorporated in setting a limit: "Instead of picking the flowers, you may rake leaves or hunt for bugs. Which would you like to do?"

There are many situations that leave a child feeling helpless, perhaps angry, and he really has no choice in the matter. Naomi Aldort, in *Raising Our Children, Raising Ourselves,* suggests engaging young children in "power games." These let them feel that they are in control, but in a playful and safe manner. She provides an example: One day a boy whose family had recently moved threw all the paper from the recycling bin around the kitchen. His father, recognizing his son's anxiety about leaving his former home said, "Oh no, the paper is everywhere! What will I do?" The father picked up all the paper and put it away, only to have the boy strew it around again. This pattern was repeated for half an hour until the child felt better. Had this smart dad chosen instead to be strict about the mess making, no doubt he would have spent much more time dealing with the emotional upset. Also, the child's feeling of powerlessness would not have been reduced. This might seem like a minor offering of support to a youngster, but an interaction like this can have a far-reaching impact.

By avoiding power struggles with kids, encouraging their "do it myself" attitude, and finding new ways to offer choices, adults can guide children to feel their own power in meaningful and healthy ways.

Power plays to avoid

Look at me when I'm talking to you.

Saying this might seem like a good idea to an adult—you are establishing your authority and commanding respect. But requiring a child to look you in the eye can be overly stimulating, compounding the stress that may have caused him to act up in the first place. In fact, he may check out completely as a defense mechanism, not hearing anything you say, and continue the unwanted behavior. Instead, allow a child to avoid eye contact while you are speaking to him about your request. This doesn't mean that he's not listening. Use short concise sentences to get your point across clearly.

Hurry up!

Always managing and hurrying children may leave them feeling tense and like they have no control over their lives. A young child lives largely in the moment and will not understand why she must stop playing with the trucks to leave for gym class, even though she loves gym class. Children under age three have little ability to think forward to the next thing. At some point between three and four a child will begin to ask, "What are we doing next?" or "What did we do first?" By four, children have a grasp of time sequencing, and then moving from one activity to another becomes easier.

During the toddler and early preschool years, adults need to assist a child with transitions. Instead of trying to hustle him or her along, build in extra time to allow for the usual stall tactics, and state clearly what the plan is. For example, "We're going out to run some errands this afternoon—to the farmer's market and then the hardware store. We'll leave soon." After stating the plan, give a ten-minute and then a two-minute warning. This helps a child to feel involved in the course of action and abates a sense of powerlessness. If a little one is lagging behind, hold hands to stay together. Saying "hurry up" only adds unnecessary anxiety to the situation.

How dare you speak to me that way!

Indignation will get you nowhere. When a small child sees that his behavior has ruffled the feathers of an adult, it makes an impression—but the wrong one. Though strong reactions are good social indicators for growing kids, too big a scene makes it impossible for him to consider his actions. He may simply bask in the powerful feelings of having really stirred things up, or cower in fear. Both cause an unhealthy power imbalance, and neither allows him to assess or change what he said or did. Instead, make a clear statement about what occurred and how to fix it: "What you just said and the way you said it is not okay. Please rewind and ask again. I would like you to speak to me respectfully." Setting a good example in this area is crucial for instilling in children the value of respect.

READING TIP:

Pierre by Maurice Sendak. Ages two and up. Pierre learns quite a lesson about being rude to his parents.

Love You When You Whine by Emily Jenkins. Ages two and up. This young child is reassured that she is loved through all kinds of behavior.

You have to share.

During their first five years, kids struggle with sharing sometimes (if not most times!). Children near age two have particular difficulty with sharing. This is normal and to be expected. It's worth repeating: This is normal. You might have heard a child scream "No! Mine!" at the top of her lungs if another child makes even a slight move toward a toy or cookie she is holding. Experts claim that at the peak of the "mine" stage, a toddler's perception of a toy she possesses is that it is an actual part of her. When someone takes away that toy, she feels the same as if an arm or leg has been taken. This certainly explains all that wailing, doesn't it?

It's reasonable to require a young child to share at times—but don't expect her to like it. A child can feel she has some power in a situation if an adult allows her to hold back something she doesn't have to share. Tell her your expectations beforehand: "Your friend Eva is coming over to play. She will want to play with your toys, just like you play with hers at her house. You may pick one special toy that you don't have to share. But Eva can play with all the others." Then when the children are together, repeat the rule and reinforce it, removing a screaming child if necessary. Keeping the visit short will also make it easier for everyone. Eventually kids catch on that sharing is the preferred social behavior, one they benefit from as well.

READING TIPS:

The Pigeon Finds a Hot Dog! by Mo Willems. Ages six months and up. A pigeon wants to eat the hot dog himself but decides to share in the end.

The Rainbow Fish by Marcus Pfister. Ages two and up. The rainbow fish feels better when everyone has a small bit of his special beauty.

Sheila Rae's Peppermint Stick by Kevin Henkes. Ages one and up. Sheila Rae doesn't want to share at first, but then something happens that changes her mind.

Go say you're sorry.

Forcing a child to apologize is usually frustrating for someone—the child who has been given no choice in the matter, or the adult if the child refuses. I've seen moms and dads have major "say you're sorry" showdowns with children who have just begun to speak: "We will stand right here until you say you are sorry for hitting your friend!" It is upsetting to watch one child hurt another, but trying to save face in this situation is a trap. Children under five are still developing empathy and don't benefit from a forced apology. The best response is to describe what occurred. It helps them understand the connection between cause and effect—you did this, and it caused that.

A great example for toddlers is for an adult to handle the wrongdoing and apologize to the affronted child or grown-up: "I'm sorry Helen pushed you and took that toy. Are you okay?" You could say to Helen, "You knocked Jimmy over and took his toy. I'm taking it away from you and giving it back to him. Pushing and grabbing are not the right ways to get what you want. Jimmy is upset that you took his toy, and he's crying because he hit his head when he fell." At a later stage in development (around age three), ask the child to take the lead with a friend she has offended or injured. This works like a scaffold to help the apology be included, which it usually will if it has been demonstrated often enough.

READING TIPS:

I'm Sorry by Sam McBratney. Ages one and up. Two young friends want to play together, but first they must mend hurt feelings.

How to Lose All Your Friends by Nancy Carlson. Ages two and up. This "how to" tells you exactly what not to do if you want friends.

Don't you say "no" to me.

A child's use of *no* is often his way of striving for power. Though many people have an aversion to hearing this from their little ones, it is one of those necessary stages of development that all kids go through. Answering a child's "No!" with a simple "Today that is not a choice" can be quite effective. Challenging a young child who is in a stage of negativism just leads to a tiresome power struggle. Instead, redirect his attention in a firm way: "I hear you saying 'no' but we are moving on now." This lets him know you are in charge without directly challenging his statement or, as a wise coteacher of mine once said, "rubbing it in."

READING TIPS:

No, David! by David Shannon. Ages one and up. David hears a lot of "no" and gets a big "yes" in the end.

Don't Let the Pigeon Drive the Bus! by Mo Willems. Ages one and up. This interactive book gives young ones an outlet for saying "no."

What's the magic word?

Most adults want children to have good manners. However, constant prompting usurps kids' personal power. We certainly don't remind and nag at a baby to start crawling, and it isn't productive for learning other behaviors like manners. Ironically, asking repeatedly for *please* or *thank you* can cause a child to overlook manners. Why should she remember to say the magic words if you always jog her memory? I have effectively taught children to use polite phrases by simply always using them myself. Reading books with children that promote courteous behavior and respect for others is another effective way to send the manners message without nagging.

In social situations where you would feel rude if a child doesn't say the right thing, rather than asking for the magic words, try this less demanding request: "Did you want to say 'thank you?'" This prompt may elicit the response you seek. If not, speak for your child (he will hear you) without sarcasm or a mocking tone: "Thanks, Aunt Trudy. Frankie will love playing with this truck."

READING TIP:
Rude Giants by Audrey Wood. Ages two and up. These unruly giants get some etiquette help.

Acknowledgments

This book has been a true labor of love. More people than I have space to mention contributed to its creation and I am grateful to every one of you.

Julia Chitwood is the most patient woman on earth for undertaking this project. Your commitment and perseverance have been unshakable and your insight and precision honed this book immeasurably. Thank you for challenging me.

Thank you Waimea Williams for your editorial prowess. What emerged after your handiwork is a clearer and much more reader-friendly version of things.

Trish Schutz-Krause added to this book immensely with her thoughtful and amusing drawings of life with young children. Thank you for your flexibility and determination.

The many children I have worked with have allowed me to learn as well as to teach. I am particularly grateful for my rewarding long-term relationships with Anson and Graham Brown, and Emil Napier. And I am indebted to their parents for giving me the incredible gift of trust while I cared for their kids.

My first parenting teachers were those who parented me. You showed grace and good humor, and knew when it was right to admit you were wrong. I greatly appreciate *all* of you, especially my mom and dad, Kathi Pewitt and Dan Goldstein. Huge thanks to the members of my extended family who have offered moral support, insightful manuscript reviews, and unflagging faith in me.

So many other dear people have aided in the evolution of this book. Among them are Daylen Jones, Maria Casey, Danielle Champlain, Naomi and Jerome Ryan, Bobbie Casey, Nancy Rosa, Linda Larsen, Chris Pasquini, José Pena, Kelly Whelan, Juliet Pekerow, Bernice Casey, Linda and Chris Newton, Gretchen Hoskins, the late Tony Harrow, Rachel Pargeter, Gay DeHart, the late Elisabeth Daniels, Deb Dunlap, Heather Robinson, Anne Hallward, Jim Rough, and Elizabeth Salin. You've given me examples of great parenting, reality checks, pertinent information, endless enthusiasm, personal insights, and honest feedback. Thank you all very much.

I offer unending gratitude to my amazing best friend and husband, Rich. Your belief in me is unwavering. I could not have done it without you. And to Joshua, my greatest delight and the best reason I have to practice what I've preached. This book is dedicated in love to you, my sweet son.

Resource Books for Grown-ups

If you are looking for more information about the topics in this book, here are some suggestions for further reading.

These books offer more insight into talking with children:

Talking to Your Kids in Tough Times: How to Answer Your Child's Questions About the World We Live In by Willow Bay. Warner Books, 2003.

What Did I Just Say!?! How New Insights into Childhood Thinking Can Help You Communicate More Effectively With Your Child by Denis Donovan, MD, and Deborah McIntyre, RN. Henry Holt and Company, 1999.

How To Talk So Kids Will Listen and Listen So Kids Will Talk by Adele Faber and Elaine Mazlish. HarperCollins, 1999, 2002.

These have useful information and troubleshooting help for a myriad of common problems in childhood:

Positive Parenting from A to Z by Karen Renshaw Joslin, Ballantine Books, 1994.

Becoming the Parent You Want To Be: A Sourcebook of Strategies for the First Five Years by Laura Davis and Janis Keyser. Broadway, 1997.

Parent Effectiveness Training: The Proven Program for Raising Responsible Children by Dr. Thomas Gordon. Random House, 1970, 2000.

Touchpoints: The Essential Reference—Your Child's Emotional and Behavioral Development by T. Berry Brazelton, MD. Perseus Books, 1992.

Just Tell Me What to Say: Sensible Tips and Scripts for Perplexed Parents by Betsy Brown Braun. HarperCollins, 2008.

Dare to Love: The Art of Merging Science and Love into Parenting Children with Difficult Behaviors by Heather T. Forbes, LCSW. Beyond Consequences Institute, 2009.

If you need a fresh perspective on parenting:

The Childhood Roots of Adult Happiness: Five Steps to Help Kids Create and Sustain Lifelong Joy by Edward M. Hallowell, MD. Ballantine Books, 2002.

Connection Parenting: Parenting Through Connection Instead of Coercion, Through Love Instead of Fear by Pam Leo. Wyatt-MacKenzie Publishing, 2007.

Raising Our Children, Raising Ourselves by Naomi Aldort. Book Publishers Network, 2005.

Playful Parenting by Lawrence J. Cohen, PhD. Ballantine Books, 2002.

Unconditional Parenting: Moving from Rewards and Punishments to Love and Reason by Alfie Kohn. Simon & Schuster, Inc., 2005.

Parenting From the Inside Out by Daniel Siegel, MD, and Mary Hartzell, MEd. Tarcher, 2004.

Raising Children Compassionately: Parenting the Nonviolent Communication Way by Marshall B. Rosenberg, PhD. PuddleDancer Press, 2005.

NurtureShock: New Thinking About Children by Po Bronson and Ashley Merryman. Twelve, 2009.

For specific information on children's developmental stages that is easy to understand:

Ages and Stages: Developmental Descriptions and Activities, Birth Through Eight Years by Karen Miller. Telshare Publishing Co., 2001.

The Gesell Institute child development series (*Your One-Year-Old, Your Two-Year-Old,* etc.) by Louise Bates Ames. Dell Publishing Group, 1980–1991.

For guidance in talking to children about sex and sexuality:

From Diapers to Dating: A Parent's Guide to Raising Sexually Healthy Children From Infancy to Middle School by Debra W. Haffner. Newmarket Press, 2000.

Talking With Your Child About Sex by Mary S. Calderone, MD, and James W. Ramey, PhD. Ballantine Books, 1983.

What's Love Got to Do With It: Talking with Your Kids About Sex by John Chirban, PhD, ThD. Thomas Nelson, Inc., 2007.

Good choices on eating and nutrition:

How to Get Your Child to Eat… But Not Too Much by Ellyn Satter. Bull Publishing Company, 1987.

The Family Nutrition Book: Everything You Need to Know About Feeding Your Children - From Birth Through Adolescence by William Sears, MD, and Martha Sears, RN. Little, Brown and Company, 1999.

To learn about communicating with infants:

Baby Signs: How to Talk with Your Baby Before Your Baby Can Talk, 2nd ed., by Linda Acredolo and Susan Goodwyn, McGraw-Hill, 2002.

What Babies Say Before They Can Talk : The Nine Signals Infants Use to Express Their Feelings by Paul Holinger, MD, MPH. Simon and Schuster, 2003.

To help you manage your emotions and guide children in managing theirs:

Healing the Shame That Binds You, rev. ed., by John Bradshaw. Heath Communications, Inc., 2005.

The Gift of Fear: Survival Signals That Protect Us from Violence by Gavin de Becker. Little, Brown and Company, 1997.

The Dance of Fear: Rising Above Anxiety, Fear and Shame to Be Your Best and Bravest Self by Harriett Lerner. HarperCollins, 2004.

Raising an Emotionally Intelligent Child by John Gottman et al. Simon & Schuster, 1998.

To be inspired about advocacy for children:

The Irreducible Needs of Children: What Every Child Must Have to Grow, Learn and Flourish by T. Berry Brazelton, MD, and Stanley I. Greenspan, MD. Perseus Publishing, 2007.

Children First: What Society Must Do—and Is Not Doing—for Children Today by Penelope Leach. Random House, 1995.

For understanding how children learn and how to better support them in the classroom:

They Don't Like Me: Lessons on Bullying and Teasing from a Preschool Classroom by Jane Katch. Beacon Press, 2003.

Anti-Bias Curriculum: Tools for Empowering Young Children by Louise Derman-Sparks. National Association for the Education of You, 1989.

Serious Players in the Primary Classroom: Empowering Children Through Active Learning Experiences, 2nd ed., by Selma Wassermann. Teachers College Press, 2000.